INTEGRATED
{ ENTERPRISE }

A RCHITECTURE

THANAKRIT **LERSMETHASAKUL**

Integrated Enterprise Architecture
by Thanakrit Lersmethasakul

© 2019 BlackBlankBlock

Publisher: BlackBlankBlock
www.blackblankblock.com
contact@blackblankblock.com

KDP ISBN: 9798672717487 (Paperback)

PREFACE

The purpose of this book is to apply the "Describe Less, Think More" or "DLTM" [1] principle, facilitating a meeting point between the author's ideas and experience sharing and the readers' imagination and implementation.

PREFACE

In contrast to other literature that merely provides ideas, solutions, or tools, this book goes beyond by integrating DLTM principles, simplifying communication, fostering synthesized thinking, and generating significant conclusions.

PREFACE

The enterprise is known as a willingness to take on a new project or a for-profit business. Many parts of it collaboratively parallel work or standalone. Would it be better to indicate metrics under their collaboration for monitoring its performance and continuously increasing competitive advantage?

HOW TO USE THIS BOOK

"Describe Less, Think More"

Titles/Chapters

Ideas/Information

Questions/Practices

Core Concepts/Content

Description | Linkage | Highlight | [Reference]

INDEX

0. FROM AUTHOR — 6
1. INTRODUCTION — 7
2. ENTERPRISE — 14
3. ELEMENTS OF WORK — 35
4. WORK ACTIVITIES — 41
5. INTEGRATED ENTERPRIE ARCHITECTURE — 51
6. INDICATORS AND RESULTS — 88
7. CONCLUSION — 100
8. REFERENCE — 101

0. FROM AUTHOR

Many ones had already told us some ideas. I just asked some questions, orchestrated their whole ideas and formulated a comprehensive view of working under the enterprise called ...

Integrated Enterprise Architecture (IEA)

http://www.Thanakrit.net
Lersmethasakul@live.com

1. INTRODUCTION

"**Performance** *is an act of faith.*"

Marya Mannes

A well-performance success needs a comprehensive lens, significant indicators, and a managerial way to achieve goals together.

While achieving goals together related to common personal goals is one of the most important parts to bring everyone happy.

The comprehensive lens is described in chapter 5 Integrated Enterprise Architecture.

"Architecture should speak of its time and place but yearn for timelessness."

Frank Gehry

How does the <u>timeless lens</u> (Integrated Enterprise Architecture) look like

?

The significant **indicators** are described in chapter 6.

*" What's measured **improves**. "*

Peter Drucker

The managerial way is crystallized as an <u>Integrated Enterprise Platform</u> [2] and highly recommended for enterprise **progress**.

What are the key indicators of the architecture needed for tracking <u>enterprise progress</u>?

2. ENTERPRISE

*"**Efficiency** is doing things right; **Effectiveness** is doing the right things."*

Peter Drucker

Efficiency means the good use of resources in a way that does not waste any.

Efficiency allows ...

- Saving time
- Saving money
- Ensuring accountability
- Providing the right environment
- Improving communication

Effectiveness means the degree of success in producing the desired result.

Effectiveness allows ...

- Identifying the right strategy
- Getting recognition
- Giving the opportunity to improve more efficiency

" Vision is dandy, but sustainable *company excellence comes from a huge stable of able managers."*

Tom Peters

Sustainability means meeting current needs without compromising the potential of future generations.

Three common pillars of sustainability are ...

Environment, Economy and Society.

Sustainability concerns about <u>natural resources</u>, <u>social equity</u>, and <u>economic development</u>.

The quality of these pillars leads enterprises to succeed in the long run.

> "**Adventure is worthwhile**"
>
> Aesop

Adventure of an enterprise refers to a journey that consists of **benefits** and **risks** along the way.

The benefit means a <u>profit or gain</u> pertaining to, directed toward, or affecting an enterprise.

It may be separated into <u>material or non-material</u> benefits and <u>financial or non-financial</u> benefits.

The risk could describe itself as the **Dark Ocean** [3] which falls under the environment of

Volatility, Uncertainty, Complexity, and Ambiguity.

Efficiency and Effectiveness

Widely
and
Deeply

related to Benefits and Risks

A frame to prove how "Widely and Deeply" emphasizes?

	Benefits	Risks
Efficiency		
Effectiveness		

The Dark Ocean:
Any unclear, uncontrollable, and unpredictable situation.

	Benefits	Risks
Efficiency	C/B	C/R
Effectiveness	T/B	T/R

⬅ Direct factors
⬅-- Indirect factors

The risks impact benefits also.

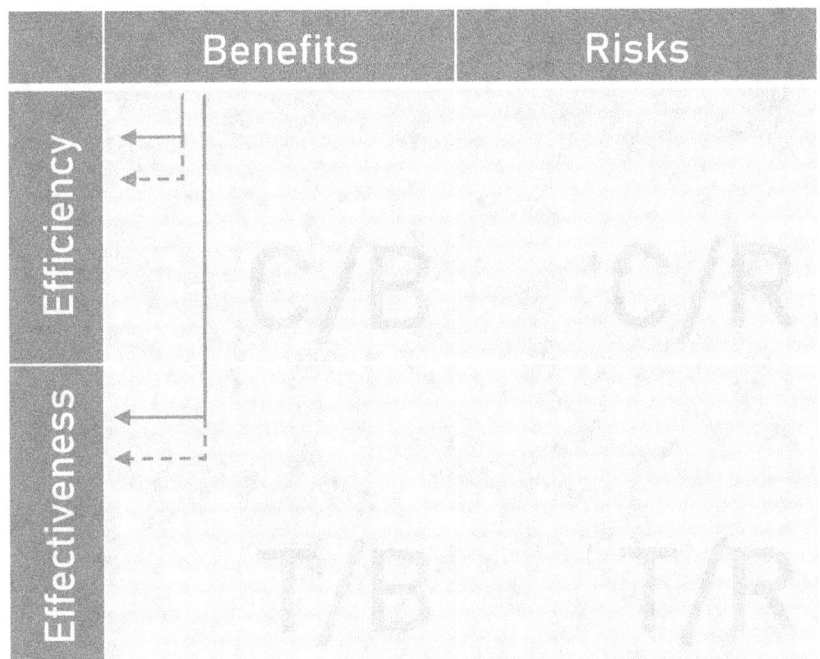

⟵ Direct factors
⟵--- Indirect factors

Environment, Economy, and Society

related to Benefits and Risks

A frame to prove how "Widely and Deeply" emphasizes?

	Benefits	Risks
Environment		
Economy		
Society		

The Dark Ocean:
Any unclear, uncontrollable, and unpredictable situation.

	Benefits	Risks
Environment	N/B	N/R
Economy	C/B	C/R
Society	S/B	S/R

⬅ Direct factors
⬅--- Indirect factors

Integrated Enterprise Architecture | 30

The risks impact benefits also.

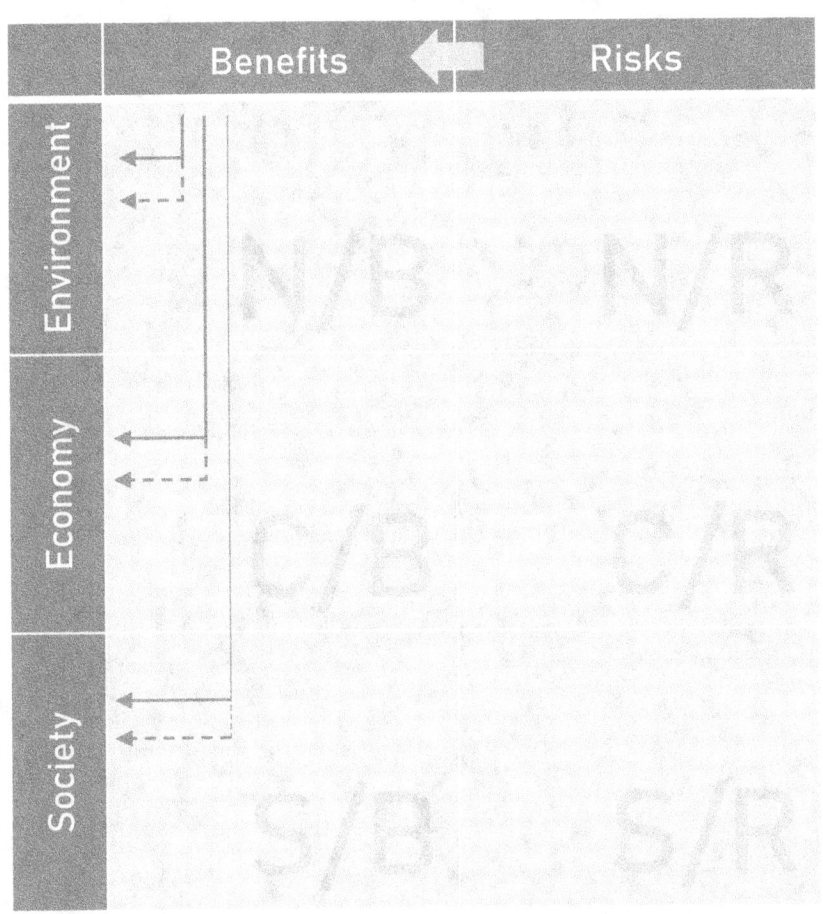

⬅ Direct factors
⬅--- Indirect factors

Integrated Enterprise Architecture | 31

What are the <u>simple but powerful</u> indicators representing <u>enterprise adventure in the dark ocean</u>?

3. ELEMENTS OF WORK

"*<u>Management</u> is efficiency in climbing the ladder of success; leadership determines whether the ladder is leaning against the right wall.*"

Stephen Covey

Elements of work includes ...

- Framing the management approach and <u>process</u>
- Managing a collaborative working <u>system</u>
- Providing a productive working <u>environment</u>
- Communicating a <u>standard</u> and working <u>culture</u>
- Organizing a positive <u>reinforcement</u> to motivate and work better

Elements of work includes ...

- Process

"If you can't describe what you are doing as a process, you don't know what you're doing."

W. Edwards Deming

Elements of work includes ...

- System

*" The system is the work of art;
the visual work of art is
the proof of the System.
The visual aspect can't be
understood without
understanding the system.
It isn't what it looks like but
what it is that is of
basic importance."*

Sol LeWitt

Elements of work includes ...

- Environment

"Sometimes a creative environment affects what happens within it."

Peter Gabriel

Elements of work includes ...

- Standard

"Safe working conditions, fair wages, protection from forced labor, and freedom from harassment and discrimination - these must become standard global operating conditions."

Paul Polman

Elements of work includes ...

- Culture

" In the workplace, we're taught to worry about what happens if we don't have full, complete knowledge of every detail. But if you create a culture and an environment that rewards people for taking risks, even if they don't succeed, you can start changing behavior."

Reshma Saujani

Elements of work includes ...

- Reinforcement

" The way positive reinforcement is carried out is more important than the amount."

B. F. Skinner

4. WORK ACTIVITIES

" <u>Engaging</u> the hearts, minds, and hands of talent is the most sustainable source of competitive advantage."

Greg Harris

Work activities are the tasks staff must complete in order for an enterprise to operate successfully.

Without the proper completion of work activities, a business cannot function on schedule.

Work activities includes ...

- Communication
- Consolidation
- Collaboration
- Contribution
- Co-creation
- Competition

Work activities includes ...

- Communication

" To effectively communicate, we must realize that we are all different in the way we perceive the world and use this understanding as a guide to our communication with others."

Anthony Robbins

Work activities includes ...

- Consolidation

"Consolidation means less equipment, less networks, and less jobs."

Emmanuel Macron

Work activities includes ...

- Collaboration

" When you need to innovate, you need collaboration."

Marissa Mayer

Work activities includes ...

- Contribution

"Every person has a longing to be significant; to make a contribution; to be a part of something noble and purposeful.."

John C. Maxwell

Work activities includes ...

- Co-creation

"An individual can't create anything itself. All of our dreams come true with the cooperation and co-creation of other souls.."

Hina Hashmi

Work activities includes ...

- Competition

> *"The healthiest competition occurs when average people win by putting above average effort."*
>
> Colin Powell

Any work activities or set of activities that use resources to transform inputs to outputs can be considered a <u>process</u>.

While a specified way to carry out an activity or a process can be considered a <u>procedure</u>.

5. INTEGRATED ENTERPRISE ARCHITECTURE

" Let all your things have their places; let each part of your business have its time."

Benjamin Franklin

Integrated Enterprise Architecture

=

4 Perspectives

+

6C6P

Integrated Enterprise Architecture is a holistic enterprise view consisting of 4 perspectives …

- Business and/or Organization
- Application and/or Integration
- Information and/or Data
- Technology and/or Infrastructure

In the business perspective consists of 6C6P ...

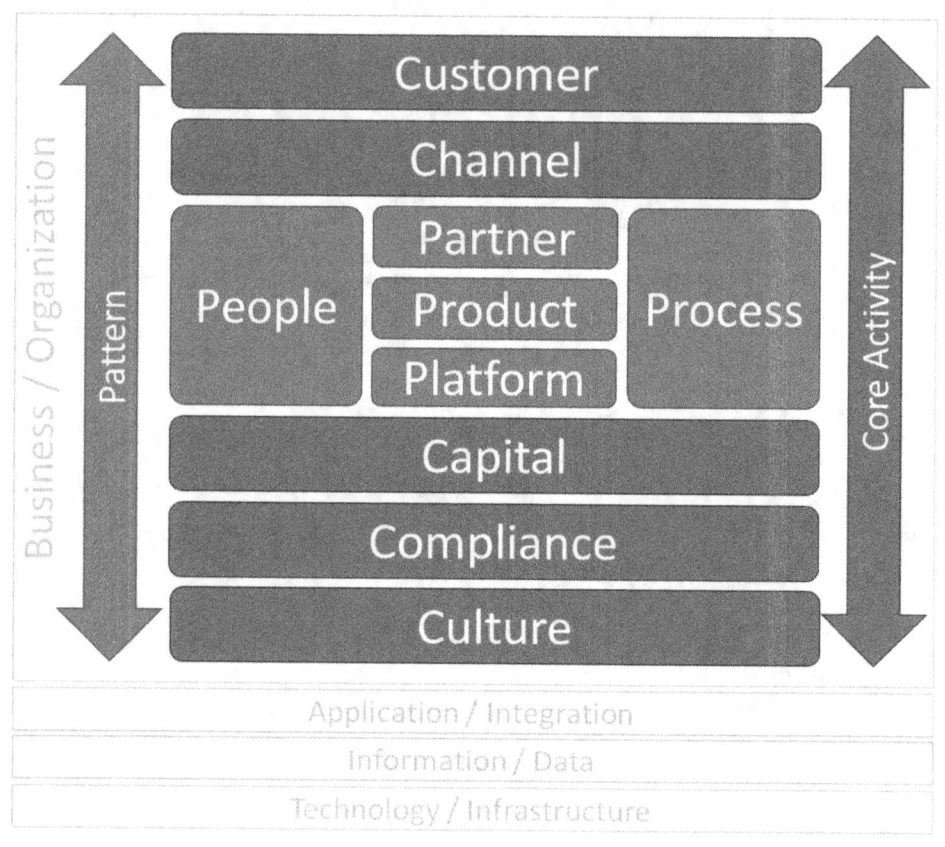

Integrated Enterprise Architecture | 54

It can be used as
a flexibility and
simplification-based
framework in design
and analysis of
an enterprise
by identifying
the significant factors
on each dimension
toward desired vision
and outcomes.

4 Perspectives

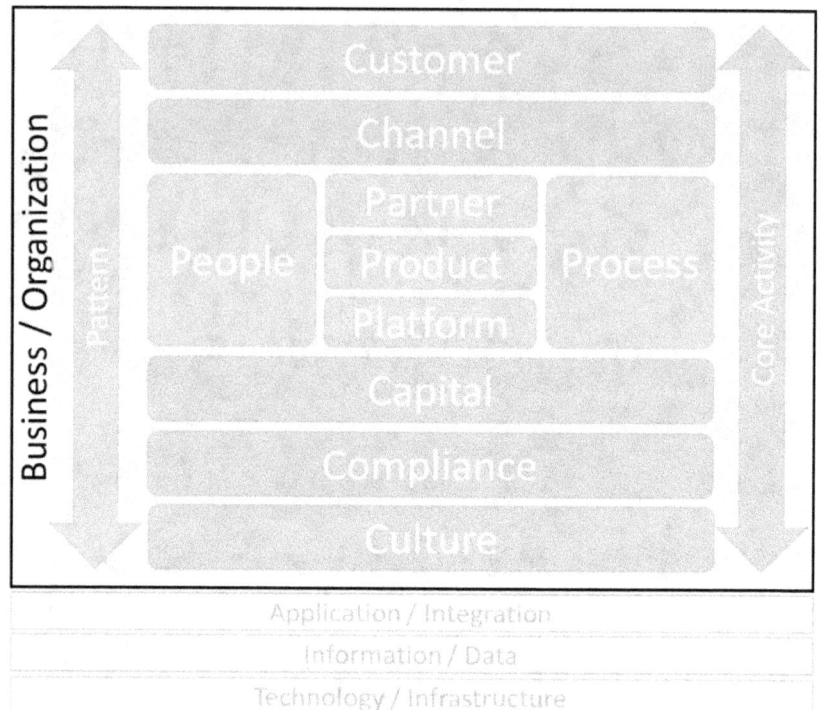

" An organization's ability to learn, and translate that learning into action rapidly, is the ultimate competitive advantage."

Jack Welch

4 Perspectives

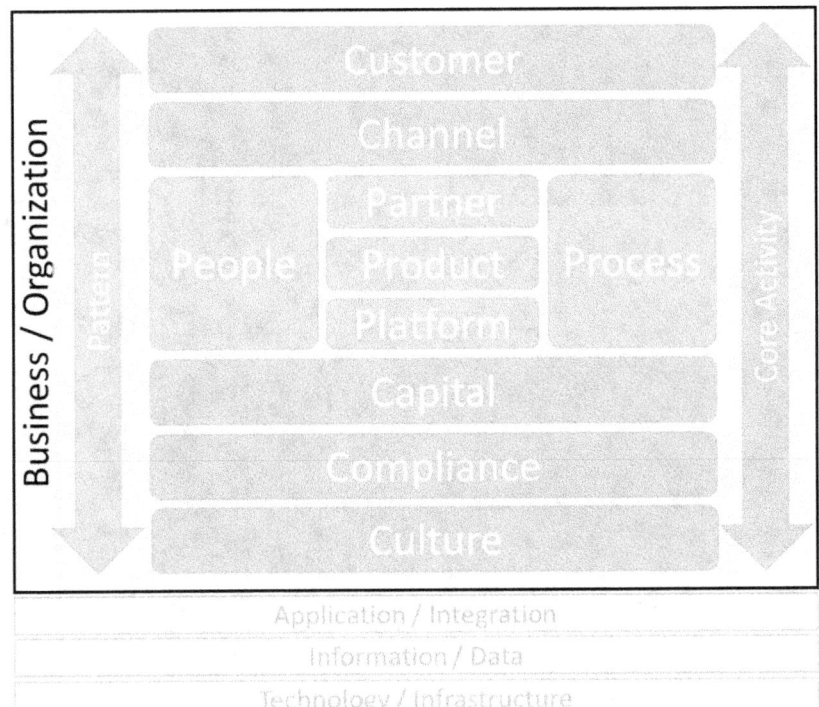

Competitive Advantage

Basic types (or factors) that allow the productive entity to generate more sales or superior margins compared to its market rivals are <u>cost, product/service differentiation, and niche strategies</u>.

4 Perspectives

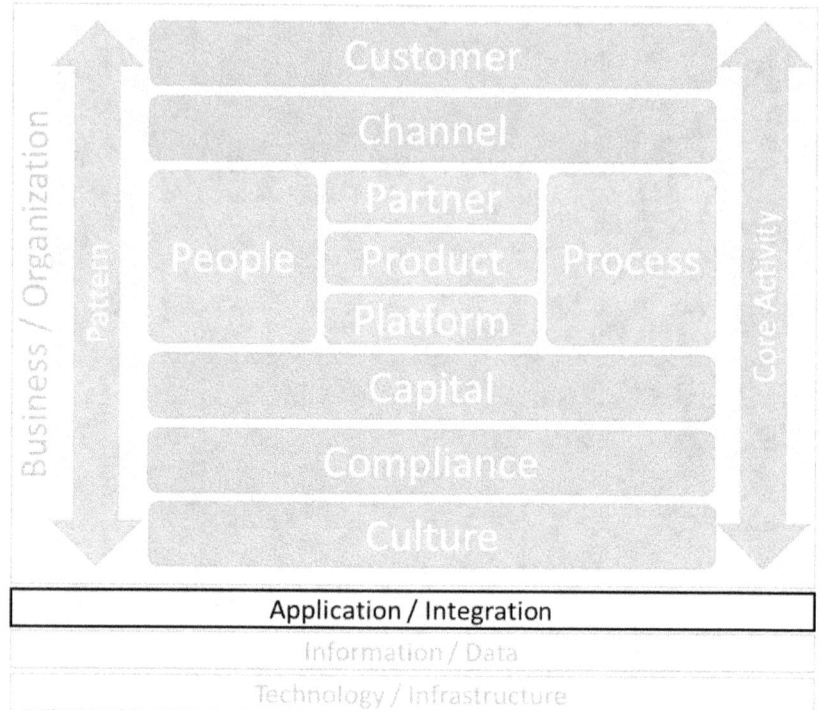

"Organize around business functions, not people. Build systems within each business function. Let systems run the business and people run the systems. People come and go but the systems remain constant."

Michael Gerber

4 Perspectives

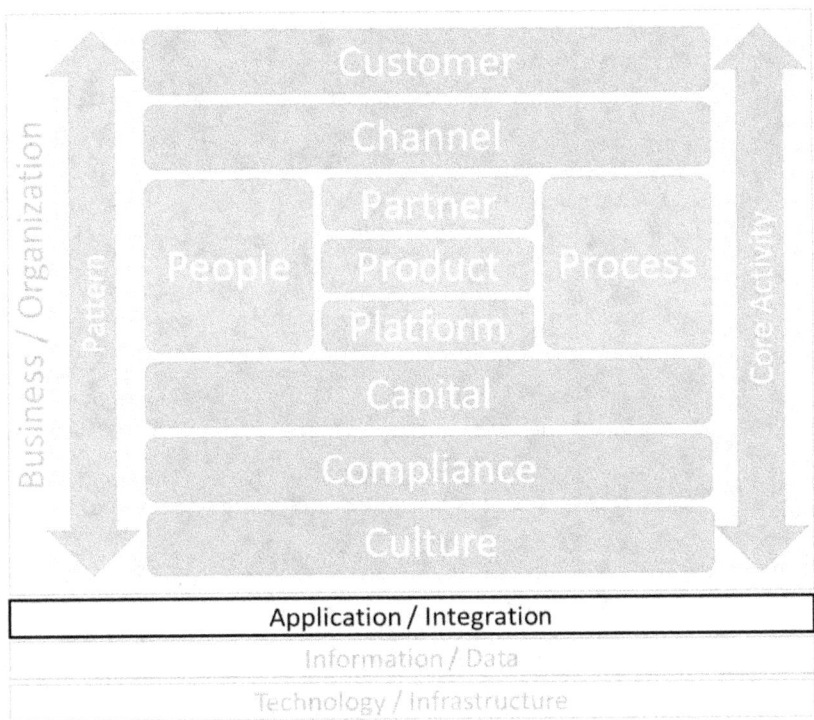

Business System and People

A business application is a collection of components that provides a business functionality with people involved that supports a business system such as <u>business planning, financial management, sales and marketing, human resources, and customer service strategy</u>.

4 Perspectives

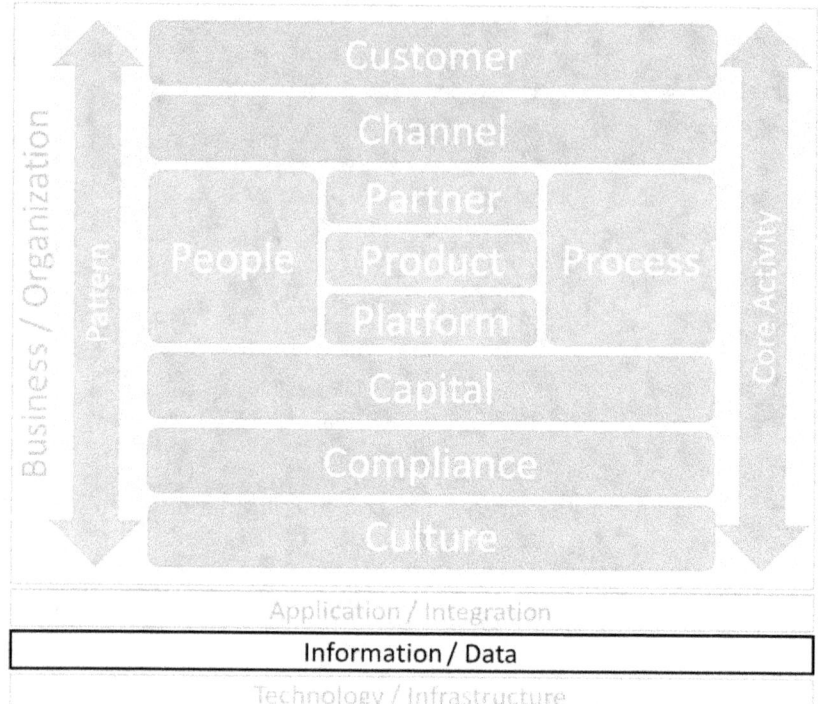

" Data itself is not enough to
create personalized experiences.
Artificial intelligence is required to turn
a comprehensive data trove into insights
that can anticipate customers' needs
and act as their digital assistant."

Peter Schwartz

4 Perspectives

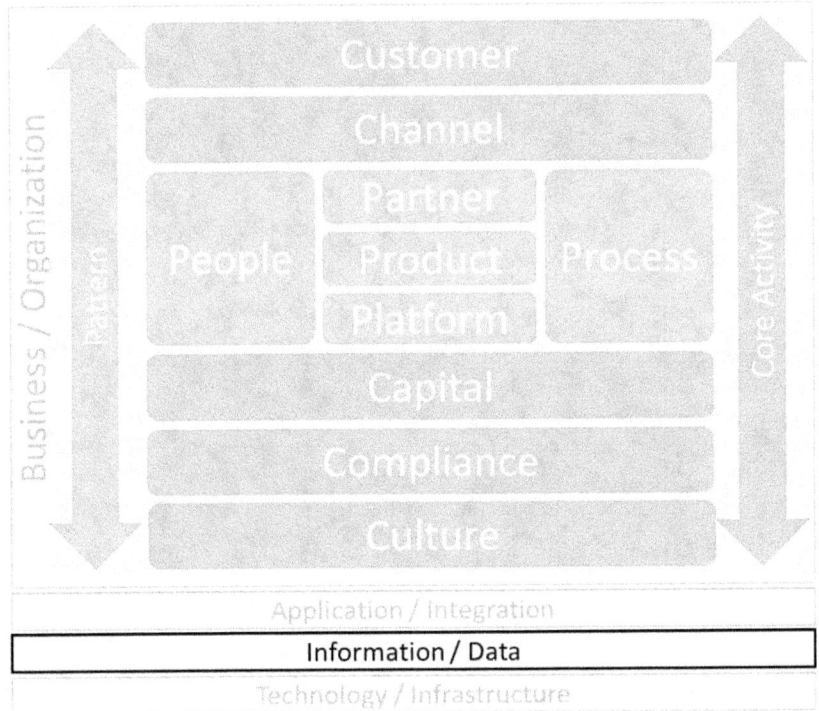

Personalized Experiences

<u>Capturing data, personalization, and segmentation</u> for designing or producing products and services to meet customer's individual expectations and lift engagement is the key to driving customer loyalty, long-term customer value, and business growth.

4 Perspectives

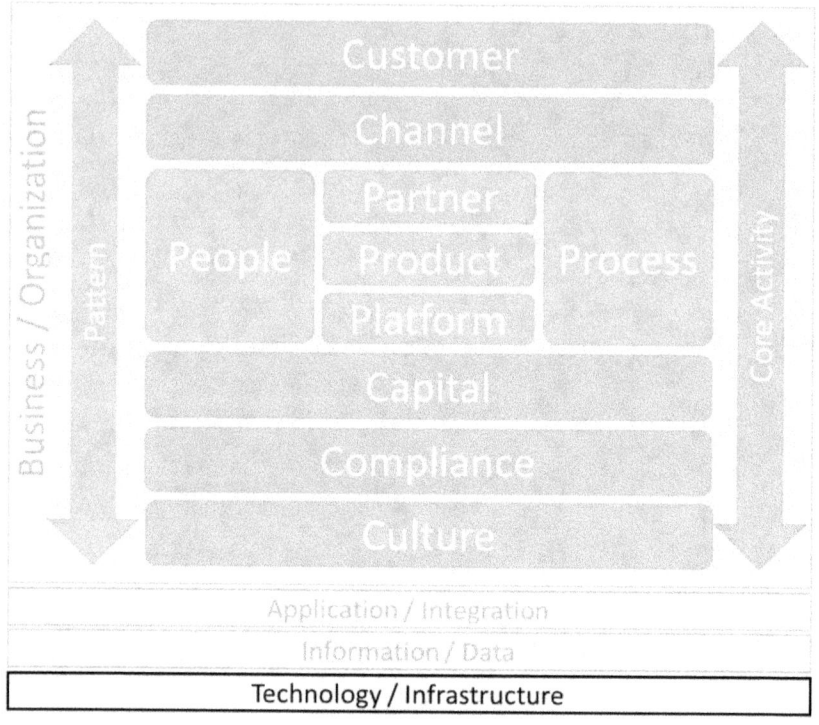

" What new technology does is create new opportunities *to do a job that customers want done."*

Tim O'Reilly

4 Perspectives

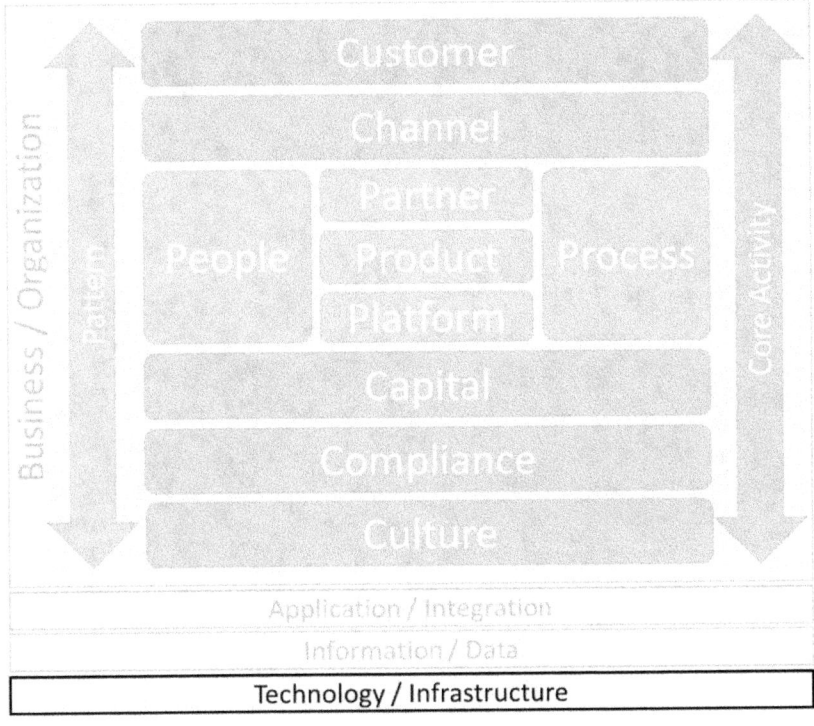

Opportunities

Technology is a significant enabler. It does not only make things easier and faster, change things for the better, but also create more opportunities. The most notable technology trends for businesses include <u>the use of consumers, expansion of automation, and scientific management</u>.

6C6P

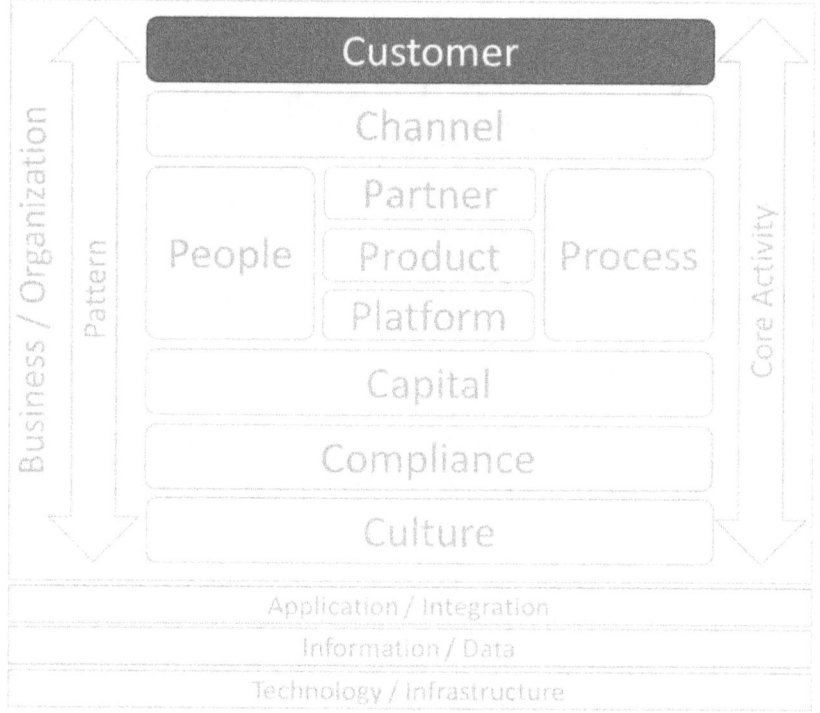

*"*Satisfaction* is a rating.*
*Loyalty *is a brand."*

Shep Hyken

6C6P

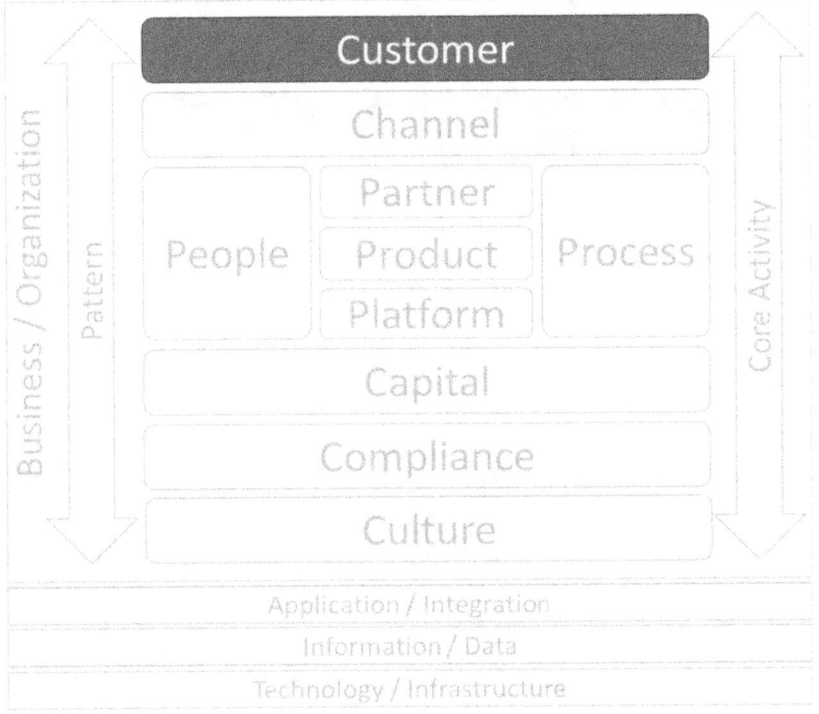

Satisfaction and Loyalty

Customer Satisfaction refers to <u>customer attitudes</u> regarding products, services, and brands. Customer Loyalty on the other hand consists of (1) loyalty behavior (or customer retention) which is the act of customers <u>making repeat purchases</u>, (2) loyalty attitudes which are <u>opinions and feelings</u> about products, services, or brands.

6C6P

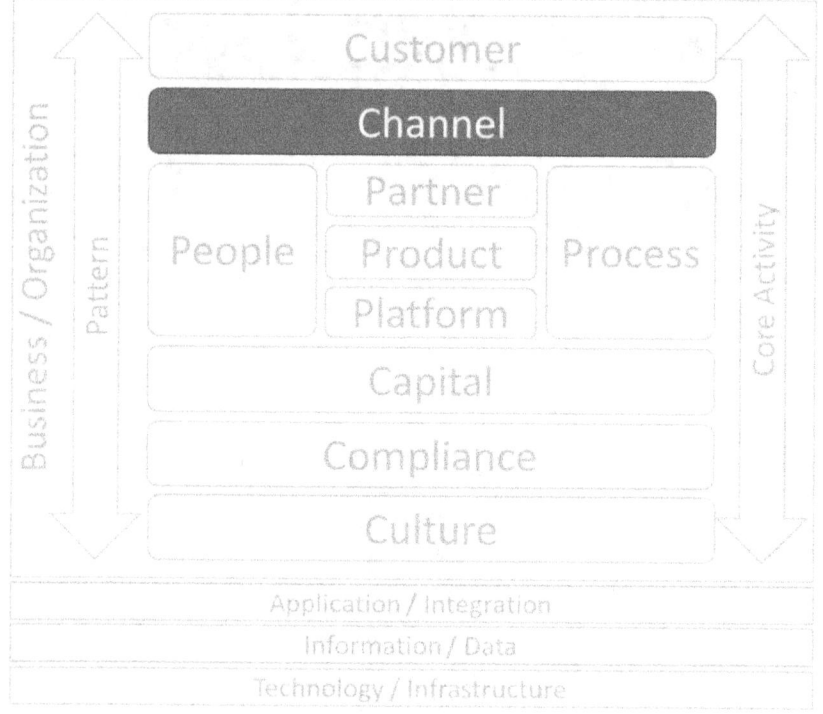

" Your brand is a story unfolding across all customer touchpoints*. "*

Jonah Sachs

6C6P

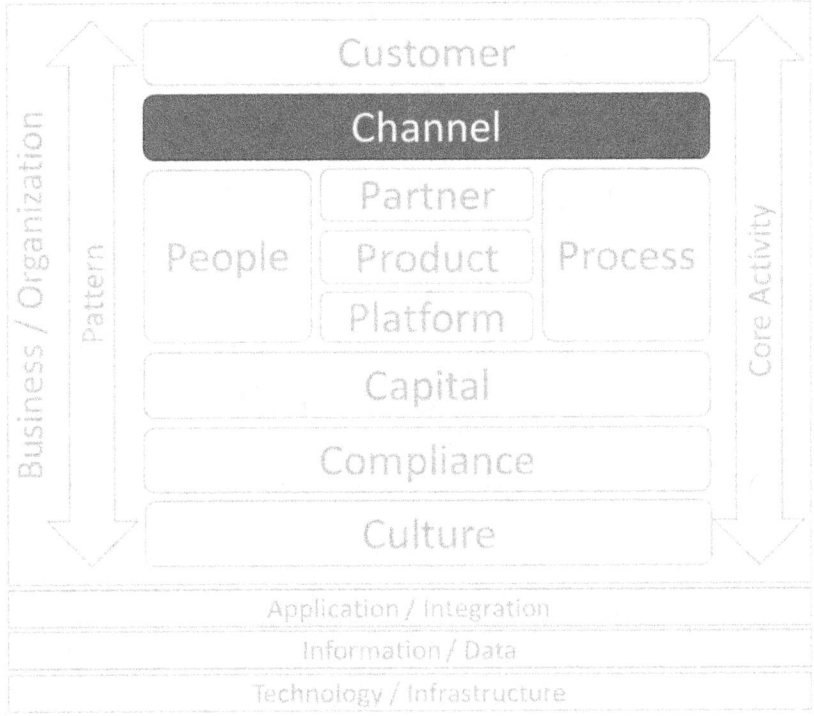

Omni-Channel Customer Experience

As technology advances, Omni-Channel becomes embedded in our culture in different ways, a multi-channel approach to sales that seeks to provide the customer with a seamless shopping experience whether the customer is <u>shopping online from any mobile devices, or in a physical store.</u>

6C6P

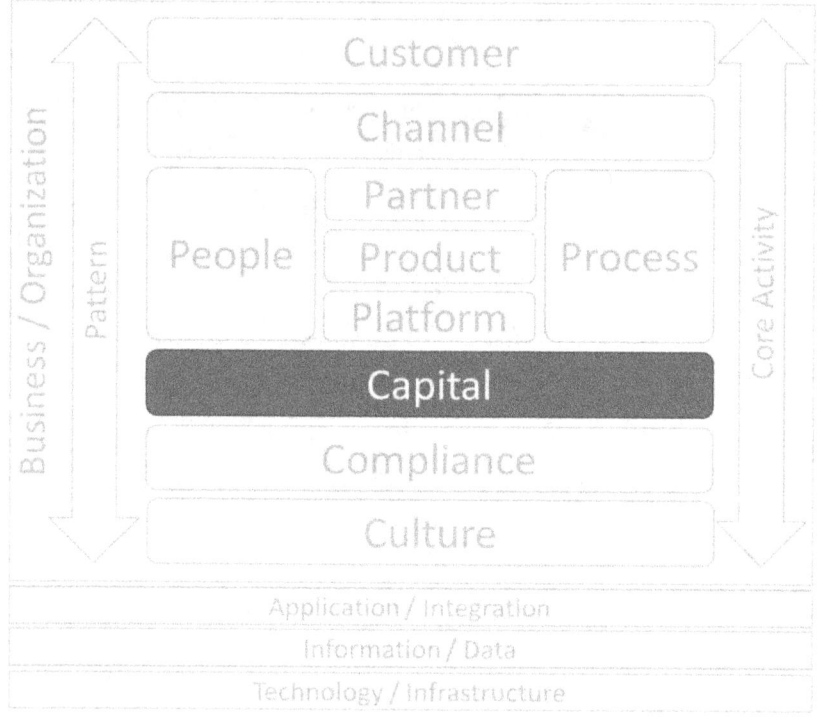

" All businesses require capital, management and labor, and business executives, wanting to grow and maintain profitable enterprises, have a strong incentive *to keep costs, including labor, as low as possible."*

Kevin O'Leary

6C6P

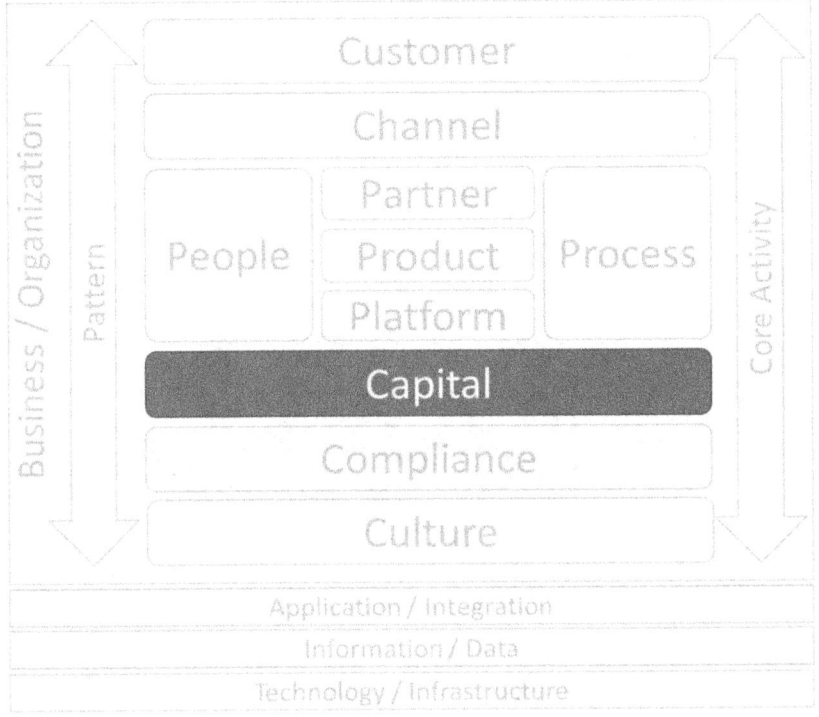

Strong Incentive

In order to achieve the maximum impact on the performance through a well-defined incentive program while also keeping costs. Monetary bonuses should mainly be used for <u>rewarding efficiency, quality of customer service, as well as encouraging collaboration and commitment.</u>

6C6P

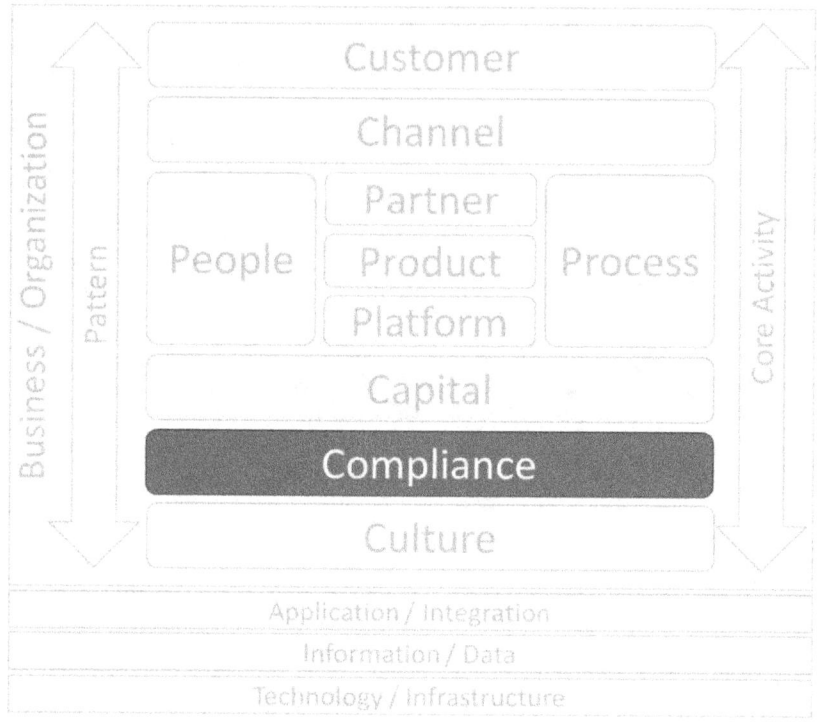

"**Sustainable change**, *after all, depends not upon compliance with external mandates or blind adherence to regulation, but rather upon the pursuit of the greater good.*"

Douglas B. Reeves

6C6P

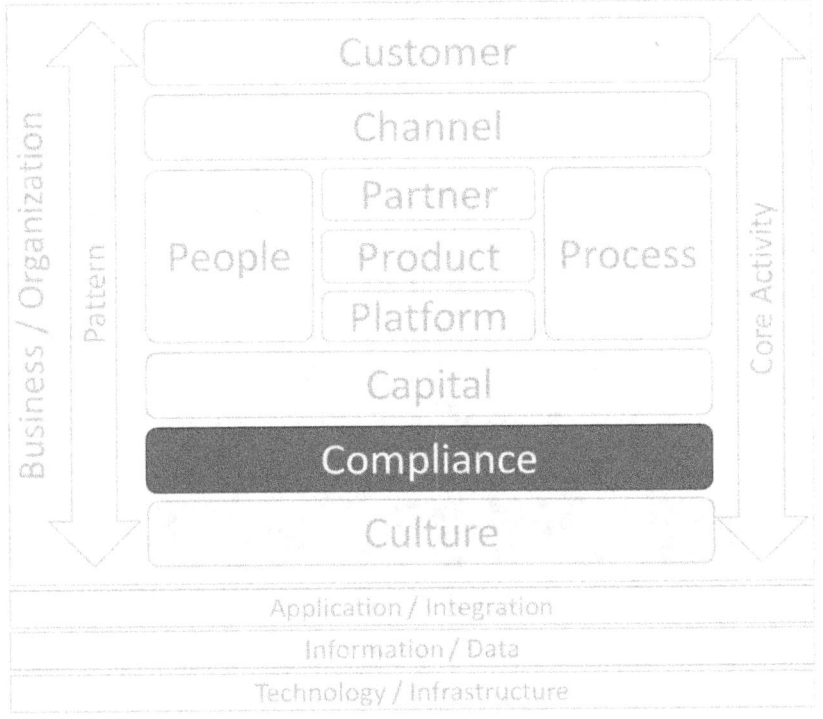

Sustainable Change

From making conscious "efforts to change" to establishing a new way of doing business, achieving sustainable change require that <u>build awareness, check for motivation, assess abilities, create opportunities, and continuous improvements.</u>

6C6P

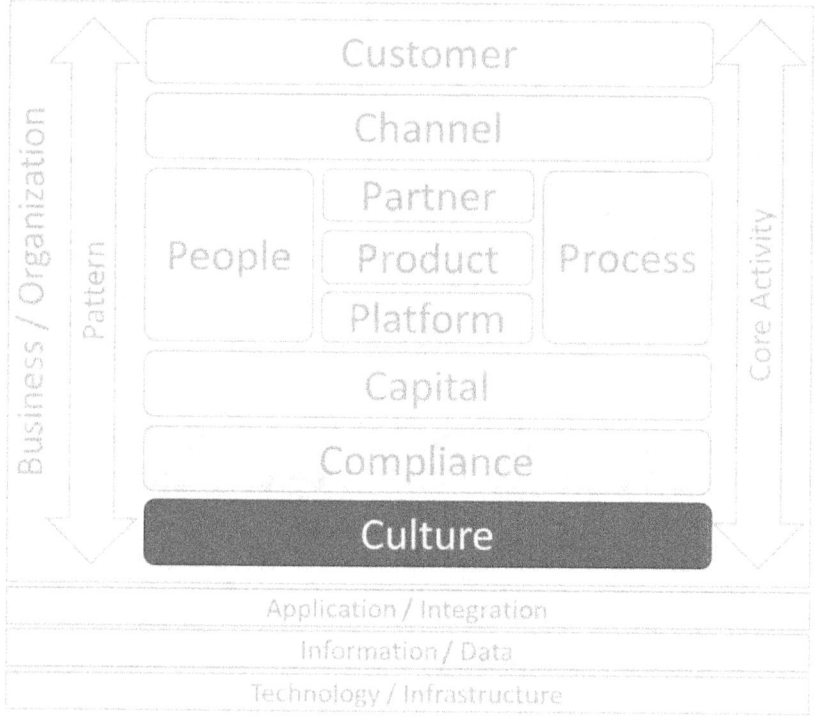

*" Make sure everybody in
the company has great opportunities,
has a meaningful impact, and
is contributing to the good of society."*

Larry Page

6C6P

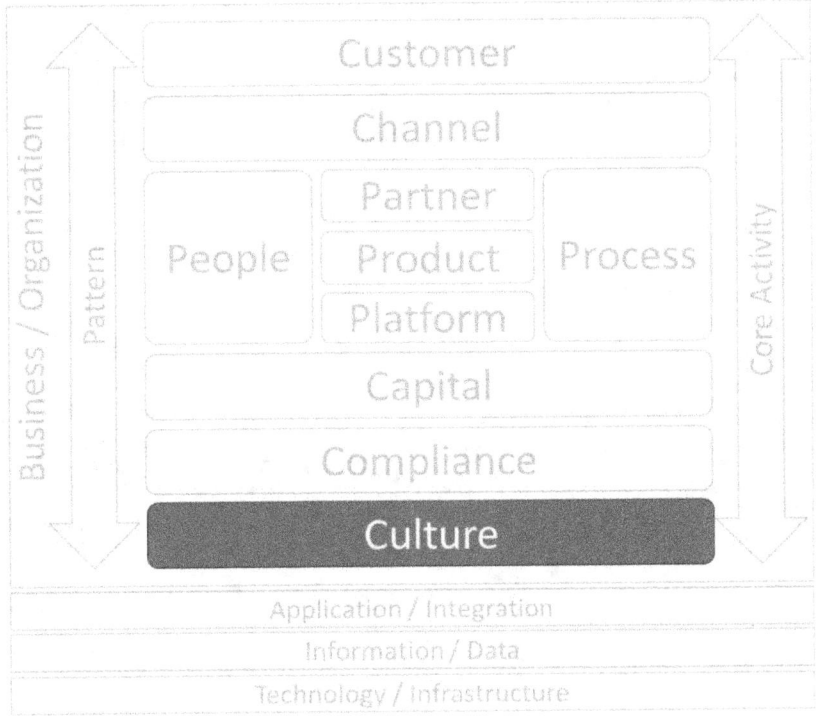

Meaningful Impact

Five thoughts on having a meaningful impact in the uncertain business world affecting an enterprise's operation: (1) Find ways to help the vulnerable (2) Decide what enterprise stand for, and what <u>value proposition</u> is (3) Learn about how <u>social/business change</u> happens (4) Realize what a tremendous privilege it is to be part of the change (5) Build environment of <u>accepting differences and diversity.</u>

6C6P

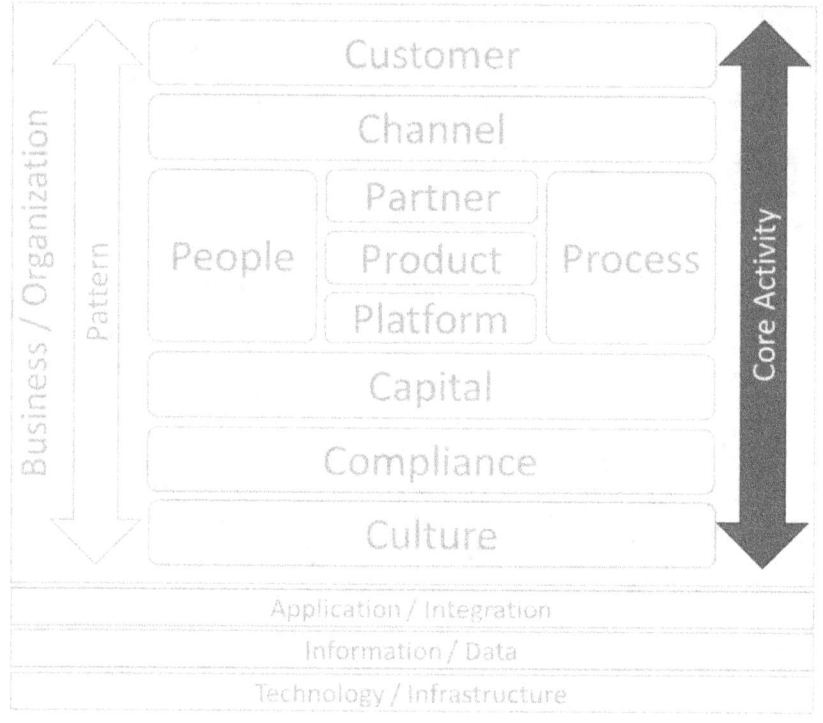

"All growth depends upon activity. There is no development physically or intellectually without effort, and effort means work."

Calvin Coolidge

6C6P

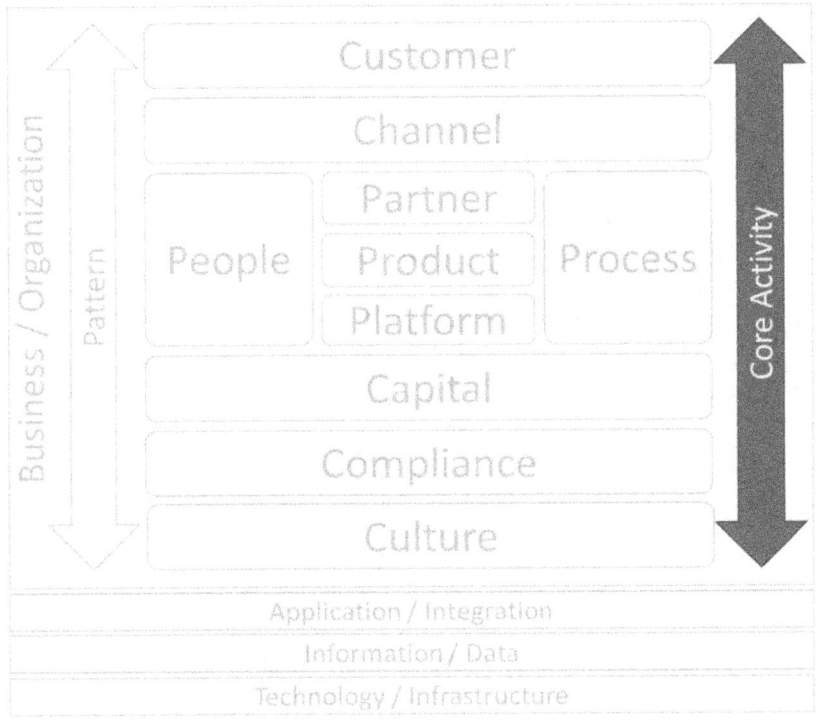

Growth

Growth is fundamental to a business's survival. Growth companies can create business value continuing to expand above-average earnings by <u>customer acquisition, product line expansions, multiple selling channels, and business partnership opportunities.</u>

6C6P

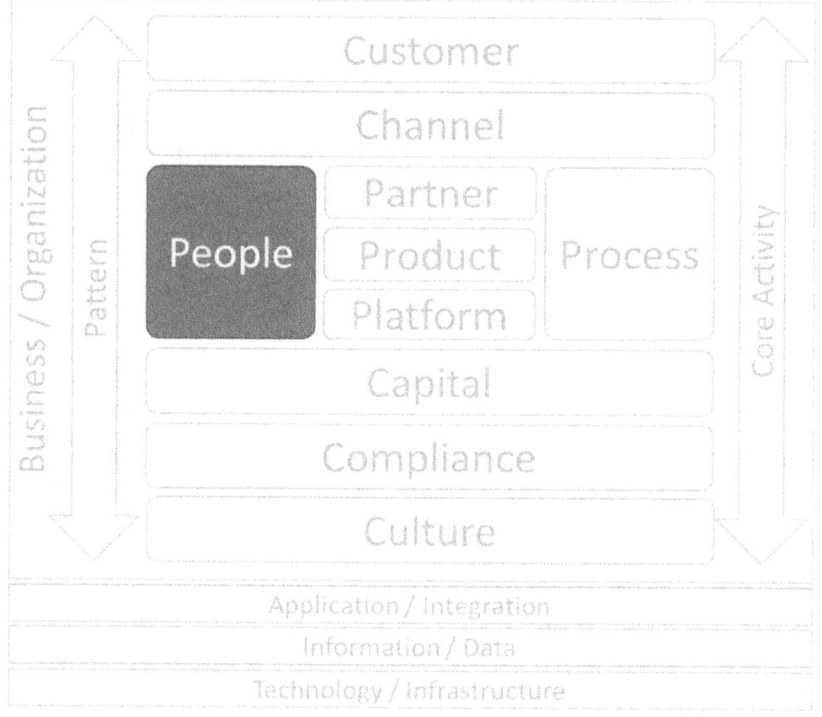

"*Showing* leadership *doesn't mean every employee will run the organization; that would lead to chaos. Businesses do need someone to set the vision and then lead the team to it.*"

Robin S. Sharma

6C6P

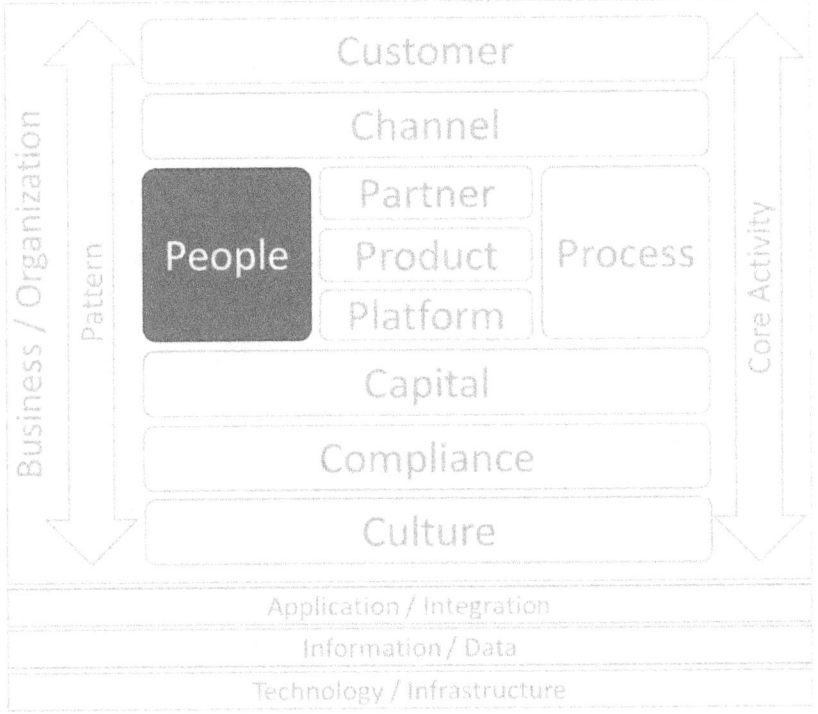

Leadership

Leaders help to do the right things, set direction, build an inspiring vision, create something new, mapping out where to go, and how to "win" as a team or an organization. Leadership can be defined based on these common elements: <u>managing and serving as a leader, people management, and opportunity and risk handling</u>. True leadership seeks continuous improvement.

6C6P

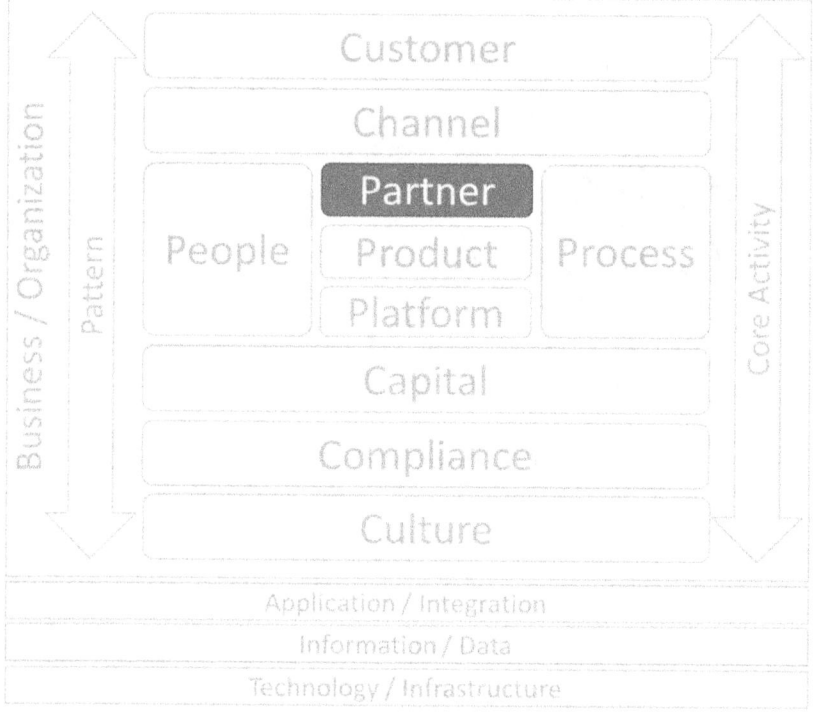

" In the long run, relationships/partnerships get falter and ultimately break when there are no shared values, or one or both parties fail to live by the shared value."

Assegid Habtewold

6C6P

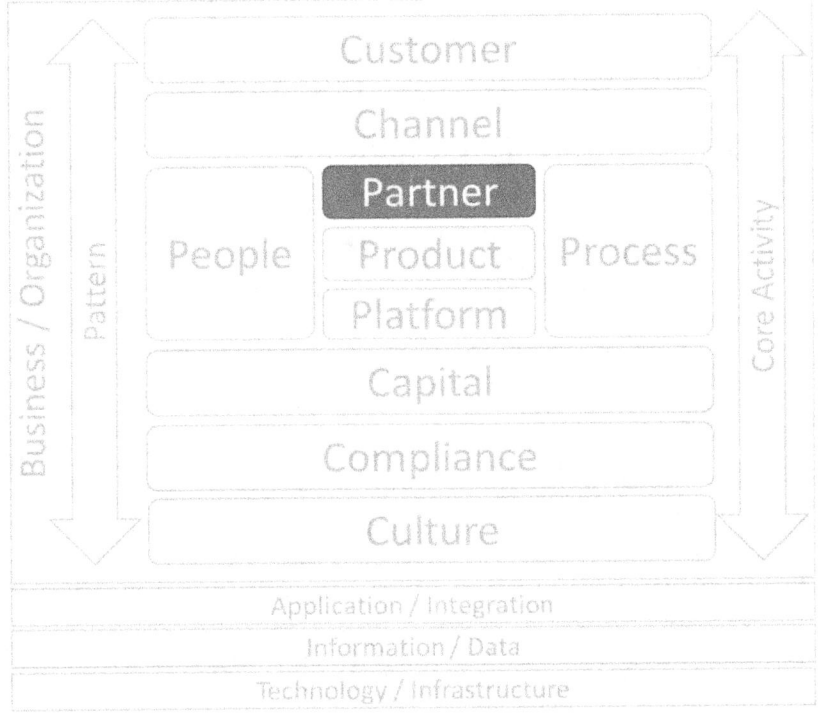

Shared Value

Shared value, the linkage of competitiveness and social responsibility, is a smart management tool and powerful business strategy to unleash the wave of global growth and to redefine capitalism. Enterprises can create shared value opportunities in three ways: <u>reconceiving products and markets, redefining productivity in the value chain, and enabling local cluster development.</u>

6C6P

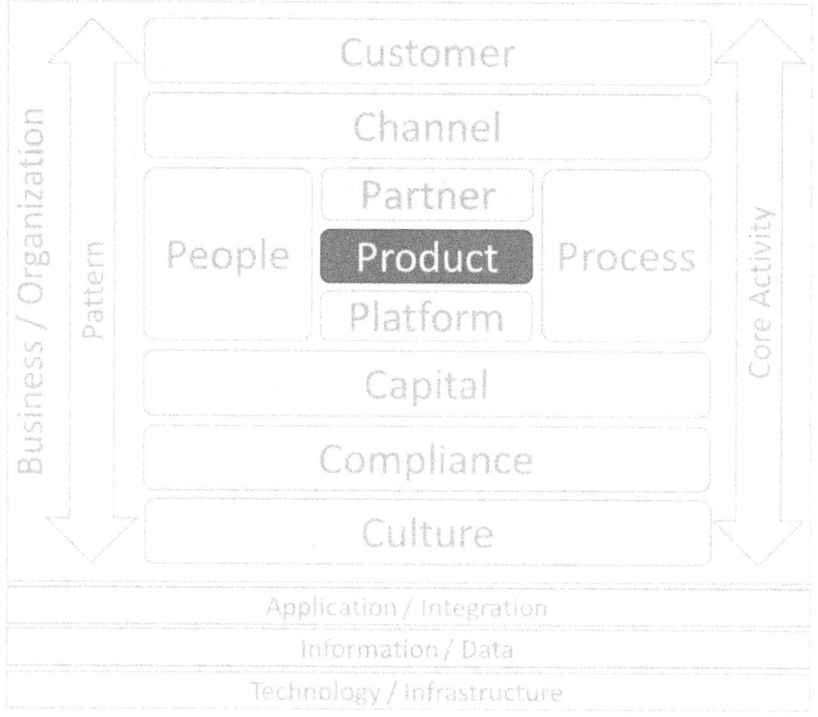

" The greatest thing to be achieved in advertising, in my opinion, is believability, and nothing is more believable than the product itself."

Leo Burnett

6C6P

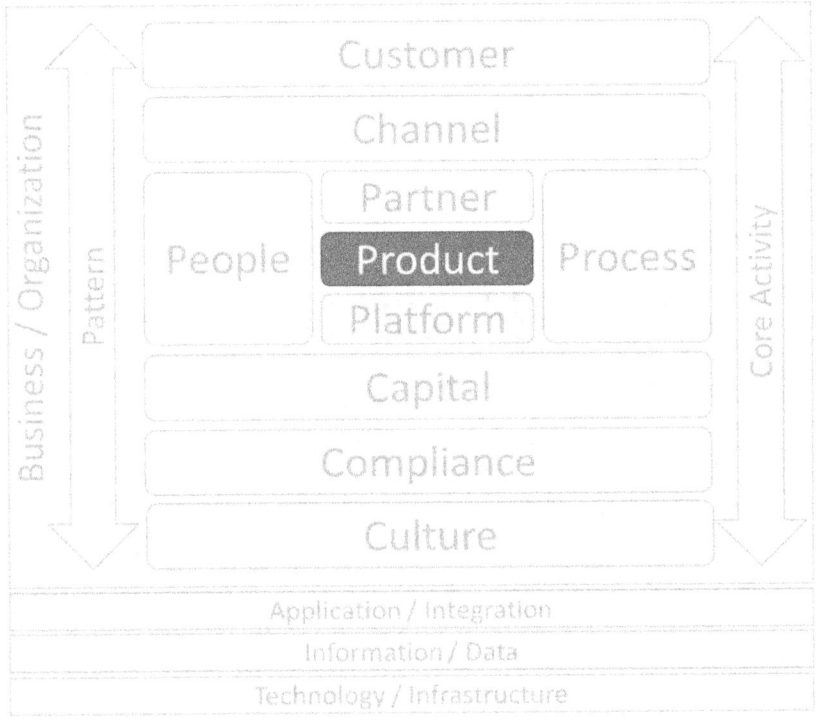

Believability

Not only presenting more product features and benefits but also proving customer experience's value and claiming believability by <u>using testimonials, converting general statements into specific descriptions, sharing the fact that you've tried similar products, showing that no competing product is as easy to use, and describing the product's popularity.</u>

6C6P

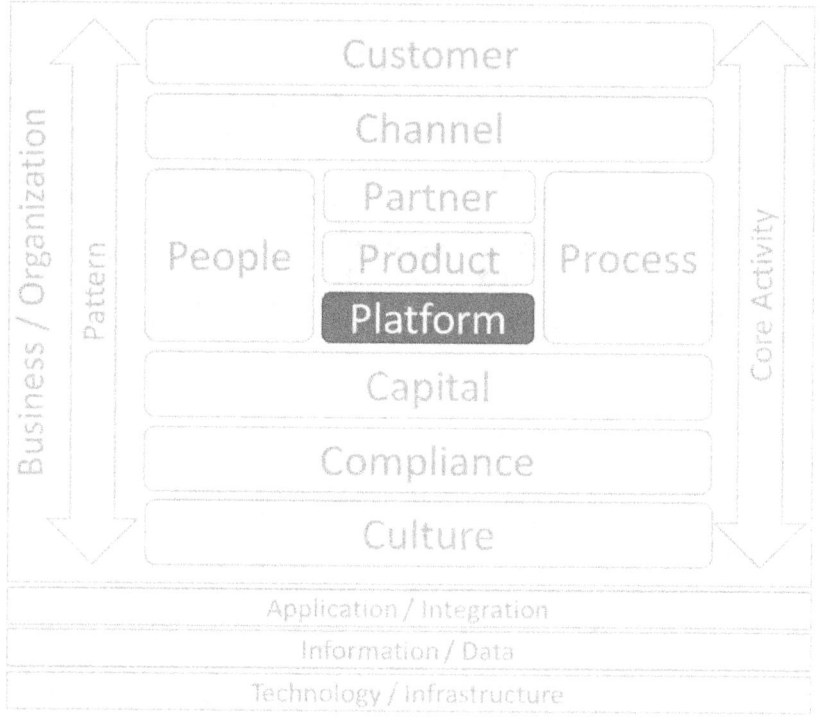

" It's urgent that companies tell their own stories on digital platforms."

Richard Edelman

6C6P

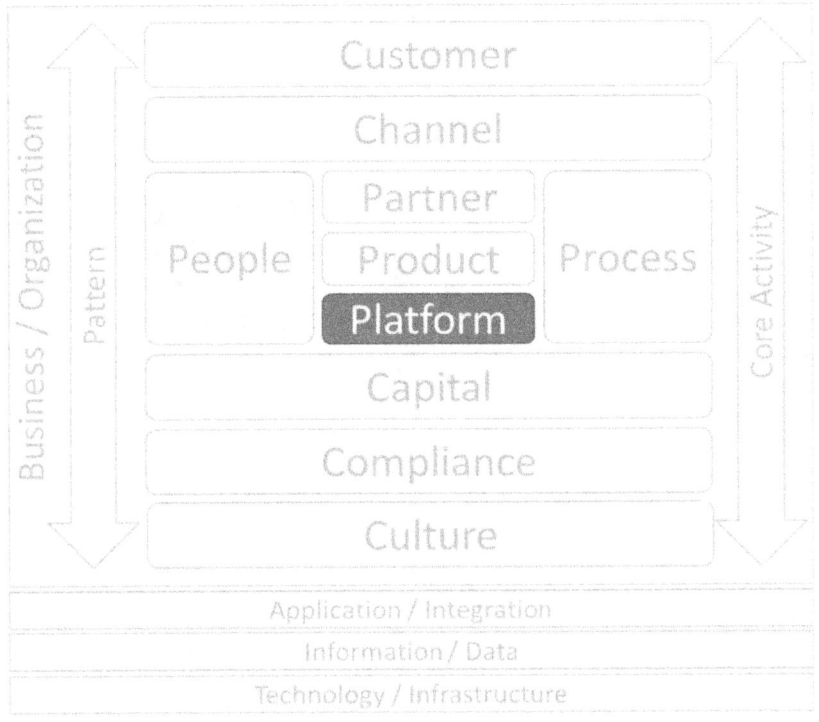

Digital Platform

The digital platform helps organizations reinvent their business models and grow from efficiency to innovation with three distinct features: <u>the network effect, the concurrence of technologies, and the open data</u>. A winning formula to create a dynamic platform ecosystem is enabling businesses to achieve critical mass and fostering a supportive enabling environment.

6C6P

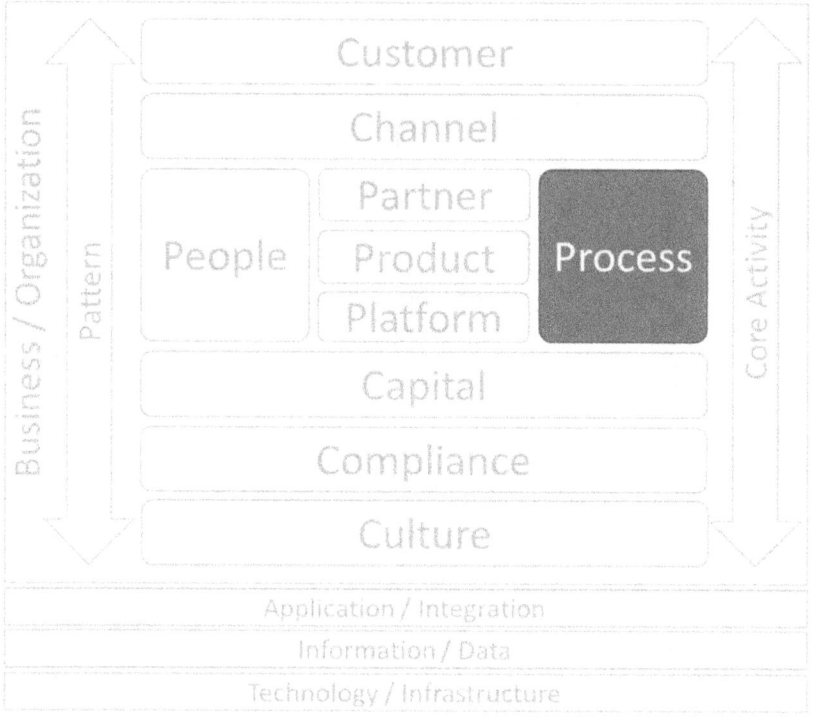

" Investing in management means building communication systems, business processes, feedback, and routines that let you scale the business and team as efficiently as possible."

Fred Wilson

6C6P

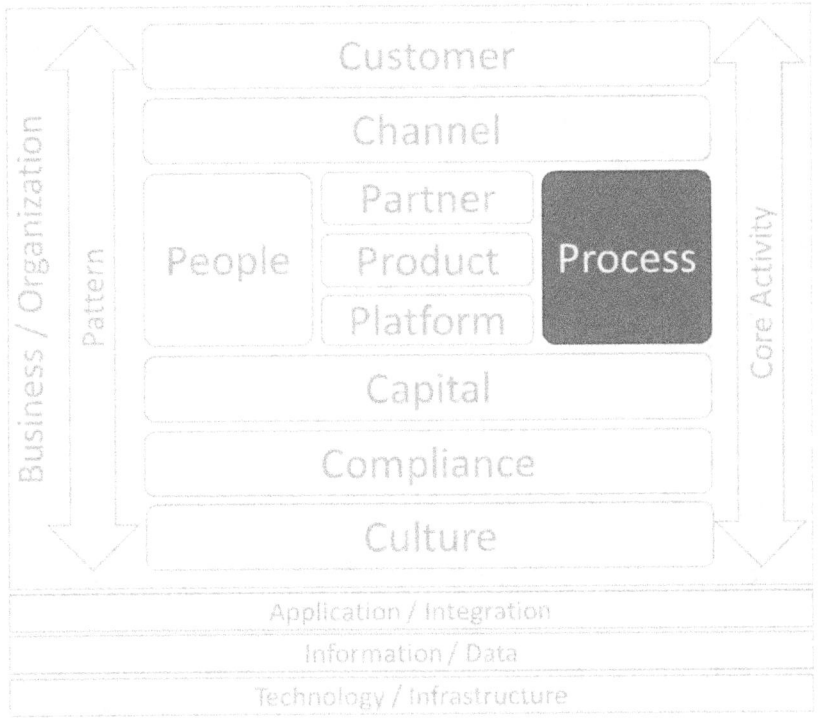

Operational Effectiveness and Efficiency

Having a high potential (efficiency and effectiveness) process is having a strong core for business. Here are some keys enterprises that can experience the impact of highly potential processes: <u>increased productivity, increased quality, minimized errors, reduced operational costs, ensured compliance, increased flexibility to changes, increased capability to innovation, and improved customer experience and responsiveness.</u>

6C6P

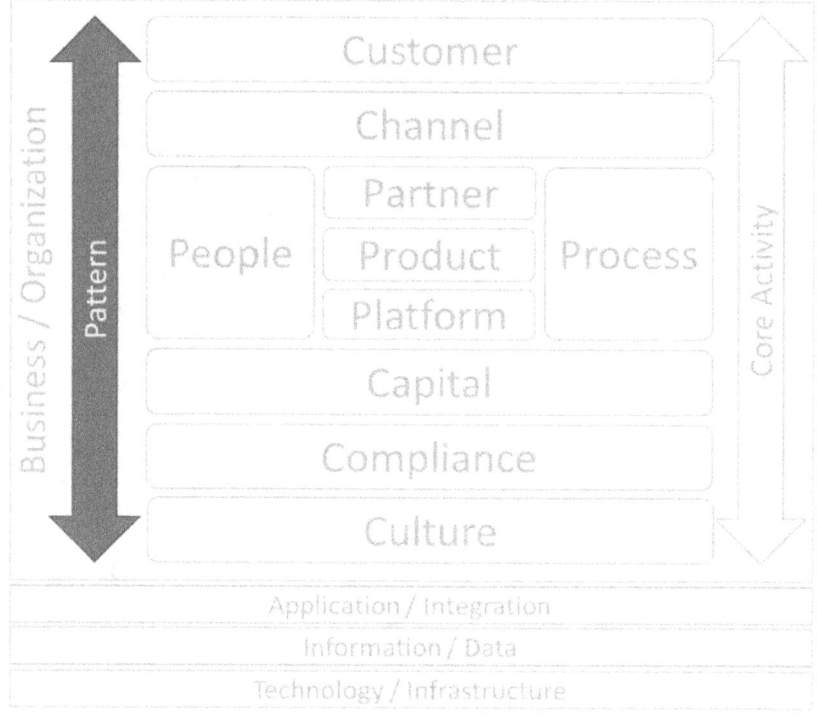

"Each pattern describes a problem which occurs over and over again in our environment, and then describes the core of the solution to that problem, in such a way that you can use this solution a million times over, without ever doing it the same way twice."

Christopher Alexander

6C6P

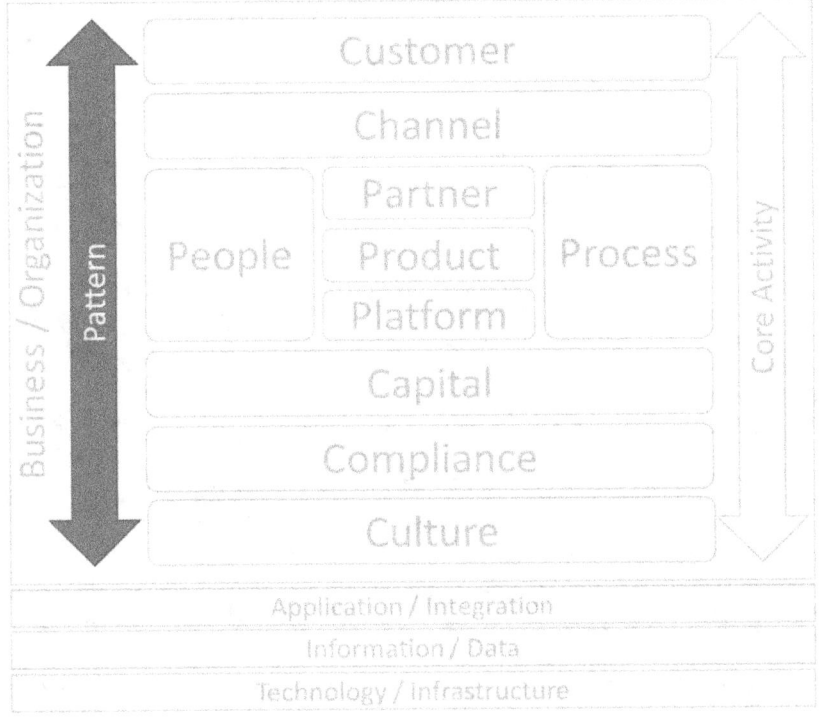

Problem and Solution

Business patterns as generalized solutions that can be applied to common problems. A few patterns that can be useful as a baseline and capturing experiences: process evaluation pattern, process feedback pattern, activity interaction pattern, and business event-result history pattern.

6. INDICATORS AND RESULTS

"In business, the idea of measuring what you are doing, picking the **measurements** *that count like customer satisfaction and performance... you thrive on that."*

Bill Gates

Any indicators and results used to monitor whether something has happened, is happening, or will happen implies at least one alternative scenario.

Indicators, or Key Performance Indicators (KPIs), are defined as performance metrics. They are applied to evaluate the success of an organization or of a particular activity such as projects, programs, products, and a variety of other initiatives.

A comprehensive framework for choosing indicators ...

Performance = Efficiency + Effectiveness
Perspective = Quantitative + Qualitative

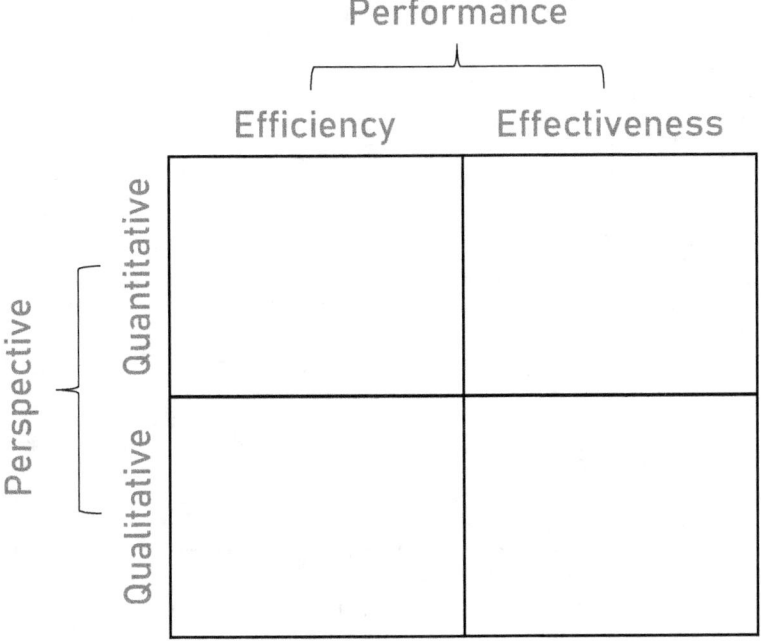

The combination of architecture and framework for choosing comprehensive indicators ...

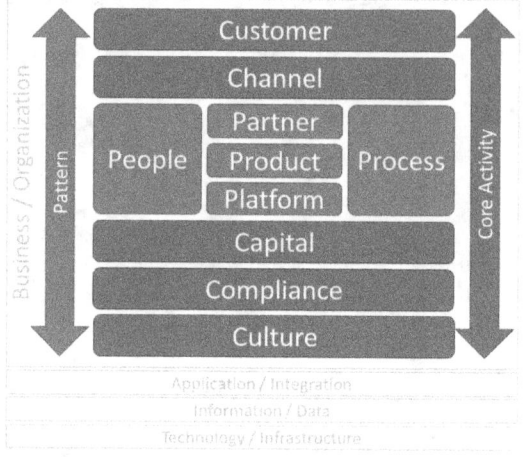

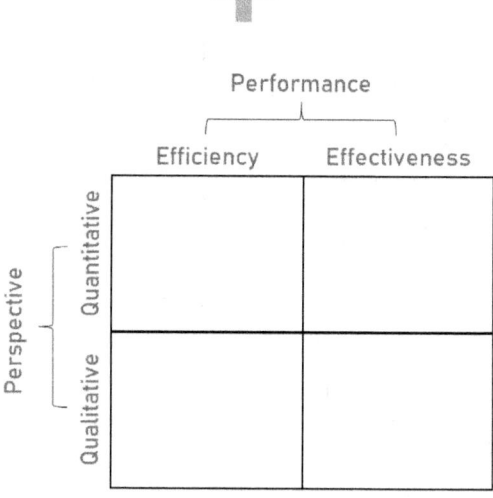

The golden rule for choosing the best indicators ...

- Start with outcomes and end results
- Make them simple and direct
- Measure success or failure in areas where most money spent
- Make sure they focus on pan-session analysis
- Segment them, do not focus on averages
- Include the voice of the customer
- Compare to your competitor

Example of key indicators

(Related to People and Process

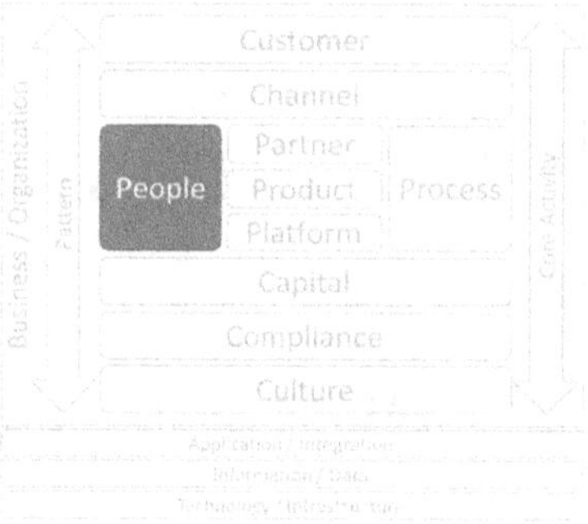

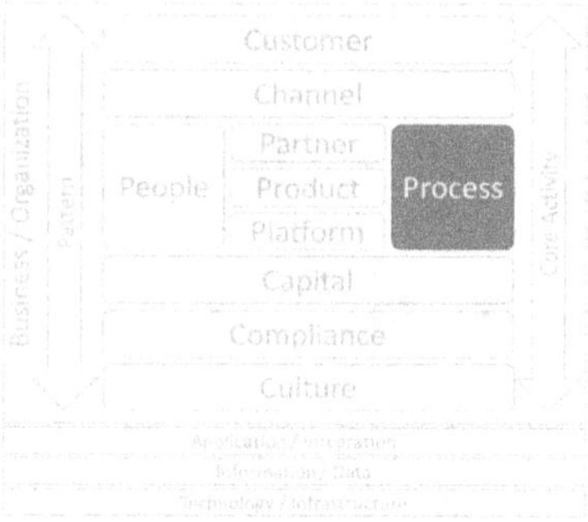

Performance

Perspective		Efficiency	Effectiveness
	Quantitative	• Human Capital ROI • Process Cycle efficiency	• Employee engagement level • Cost of managing processes
	Qualitative	• Handling time, contact quality, etc. • Ability to analyze and explain issues	• Management by objectives • Non-conforming output to total output

Results, or **Objectives and Key Results (OKRs)**, are defined as a measurable "key results" metric that defines the achievement of each objective of the company and team. They represent aggressive goals and define the measurable steps to achieving those goals.

Good practices for setting the best results ...

- Customers come first
- Don't skimp on ambition
- Link objectives and key results to company goals
- Just enough objectives and key results are enough
- If you can't measure it, it's not a good key result
- Key results are outcomes, not tasks
- Assign key results owners

Example of key results
(Related to Customer, Channel, and Core Activity)

Company OKR

- **Objective: Increase brand recognition and awareness**

- Key Result 1: Increase media engagement by 50%
- Key Result 2: Launch customer referral program within 30 days
- Key Result 3: Increase social media reach by 50%
- Key Result 4: Extend 2 new target markets

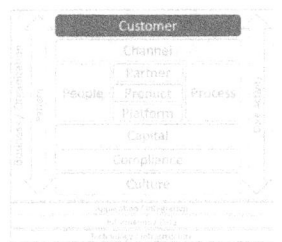
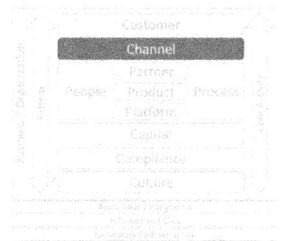

Example of key results

Marketing Team OKR

- **Objective: Increase social media engagement by 50%**

- Key Result 1: Research and identify 5 most popular social media sites and two new target audiences
- Key Result 2: Initiate engagement strategy within 30 days
- Key Result 3: Respond to all social media comments within 6 hours
- Key Result 4: Increase the number of followers on Facebook by 20%

Example of key results

Individual OKR

- **Objective: Increase the number of social media connections by 30%**

- Key Result 1: Increase posting frequency on Facebook to 5x daily
- Key Result 2: Establish 2 new social media sites: LinkedIn and Quora
- Key Result 3: Join 5 groups on LinkedIn with at least 2,500 members and leave comments on any popular discussions
- Key Result 4: Gain 15 followers on Quora by posting 1 questions and 2 answers daily

7. CONCLUSION

Adventure in the Dark Ocean

Work activities include
- Communication
- Consolidation
- Collaboration
- Contribution
- Co-creation
- Competition

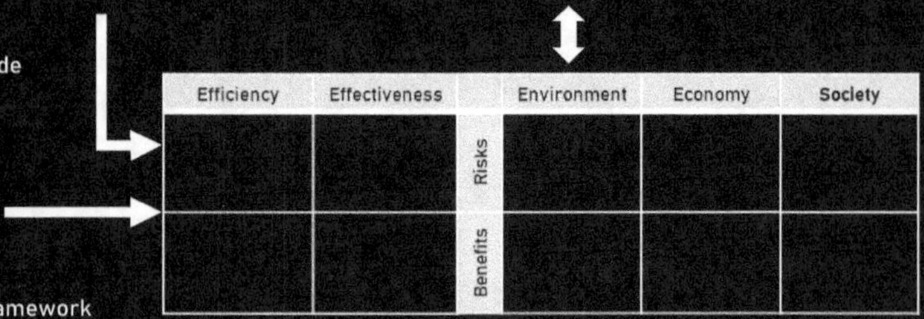

A comprehensive framework for choosing indicators

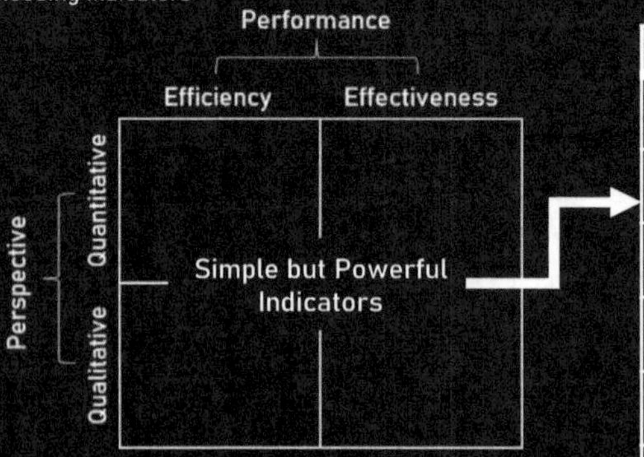

Elements of work includes process, system, environment, standard, culture, and reinforcement

	Efficiency	Effectiveness		Environment	Economy	Society
			Risks			
			Benefits			

Simple but Powerful Indicators

Performance: Efficiency / Effectiveness
Perspective: Quantitative / Qualitative

Integrated Enterprise Architecture (The Timeless Lens)

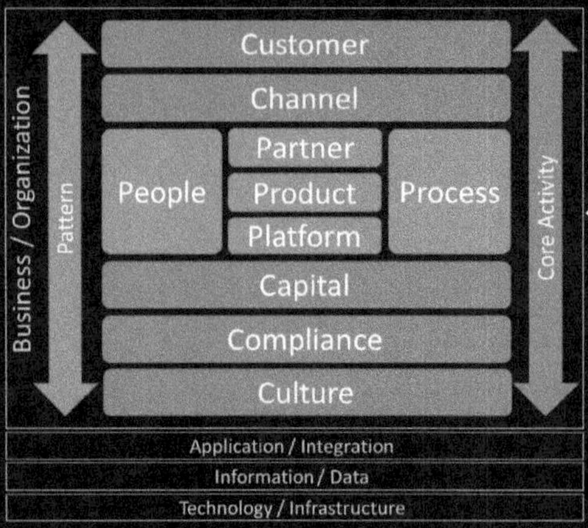

Business / Organization — Pattern
Core Activity

Layers: Customer, Channel, Partner, People, Product, Platform, Process, Capital, Compliance, Culture
Foundation: Application / Integration, Information / Data, Technology / Infrastructure

Dimensions	Key Points
Business / Organization	Competitive Advantage
Application / Integration	Business System and People
Information / Data	Personalized Experiences
Technology / Infrastructure	Opportunities
Customer	Satisfaction and Loyalty
Channel	Omni-Channel Customer Experience
Capital	Strong Incentive
Compliance	Sustainable Change
Culture	Meaningful Impact
Core Activity	Growth
People	Leadership
Partner	Shared Value
Product	Believability
Platform	Digital Platform
Process	Operational Effectiveness and Efficiency
Pattern	Problem and Solution

Integrated Enterprise Architecture | 100

8. REFERENCE

[1] DLTM: Describe Less Think More

[2] Integrated Enterprise Platform

[3] Dark Ocean Strategy

{ "Carry on any enterprise as if all future success depended on it."
— Cardinal Richelieu }

DLTM

www.ingramcontent.com/pod-product-compliance
Lightning Source LLC
Chambersburg PA
CBHW071127240526
45465CB00024B/1544